JUNK
CITY

Barbara Anderson

JUNK CITY

The National Poetry Series
Selected by Robert Pinsky

Persea Books
New York

Acknowledgments

Some of these poems have been published in the following
magazines, to whose editors grateful acknowledgment is made:
*Antaeus, The Black Warrior Review, Crazyhorse, The Iowa
Review, The Missouri Review, North American Review, Porch,
Raccoon, The Sonora Review, Telescope,* and *Tendril.* A few of
these poems first appeared in *Ordinary Days,* a limited edition
chapbook published by Porch Press. Acknowledgment is also made
to Macmillan Publishing Co., Inc. for permission to reprint "There
and Here" which appeared in *Extended Outlooks,* an anthology of
contemporary women writers.

Immense gratitude to Stanford University for a Stegner Fellowship
in poetry and the National Endowment for the Arts for a grant.

Special thanks to Julie Willson, Steve Orlen, Boyer Rickel, Rich
Cummins, and Jon for their help and support.

B.A.

Library of Congress Cataloging-in-Publication Data
Anderson, Barbara, 1947–
   Junk city.

   (National poetry series)
   I. Title. II. Series.
PS3551.N356J8   1987   811'.54   87-2417
ISBN 0-89255-119-4
ISBN 0-89255-120-8 (pbk.)

Designed by Peter St. John Ginna
Set in Bodoni by Keystrokes, Lenox, Massachusetts
Printed by Capital City Press, Montpelier, Vermont

First Edition

CONTENTS

For my Family

One

The Subject of My Pain

THERE AND HERE

Someone's lost and someone turns on
the light. In the middle of the night

the boy rushes into his parents' room
but *they* are not there;

only the rustle
of his mother's nightdress as she packs

his father's shirts, and books, binoculars,
and the paperweight—faces of the old poets

magnified under glass: Coleridge,
Wordsworth, Tennyson, Whitman,

a gift from the woman they argued about
when his father returned from a trip.

"Thank you" the woman had written
on the note with the hotel letterhead.

His mother packs that away too, and what is hers
in another carton and the child's in a third,

and the words THERE and HERE in thick black print
on a lined tablet from the first year

he learned to read; his teacher
wanted him to know the difference,

[3]

the distance from school to home
from this morning to afternoon

when he fell asleep for so long
he thought no one could find him,

until his mother took him out
to feed the ducks in the park.

Really she wanted to tell him
that now he'll have two homes.

One here and the other there,
and her finger pointed away

towards the mountains on the other side
of town. "There in that direction."

He didn't cry and his mother bought him
metal soldiers and cannons

that shot out if you pulled a lever,
soon they would be packed away

or broken. Isn't childhood
really a form of insanity? said his mother's new friend.

and the night to come when he would sit
with his father and look down through the binoculars

to the city lights—
a place that is neither here nor there.

JUNK CITY

This morning when I asked my mother
why I pee in my sleep she said
not to worry. It's just a mystery;
it's not anything. Just a mystery
like whether there's a god or not
or whether people came from the ocean or not.
My dad believes something like that.
He lives in the desert and drinks red wine,
and lets me sleep with him
and *we* don't pee in our bed.
But my mother likes to sleep alone,
sometimes I hear her praying
through the walls in a constant voice,
like she's saying the alphabet,
talking to herself like she's singing
to a baby and she knows I hate babies.

Today at school Greg and I were talking
about making a city of garbage,
a kind of Junk City of rusted nails, bent paper clips,
ripped up bushes that no one wants.
Last night I had a dream
about a scavenger hunt in Junk City
where everything was dead and we were looking
for something alive like a walking screwdriver
or a buffalo. There were shoes starving
of starvation. A dinosaur could be alive
and so could a broken chair,
but a kid could be dead. It was like that.

It was raining hard outside and I kept on
being thirsty, but when I went back to sleep
I was in Junk City again making something dead
or alive whenever I wanted it.
I could be born in 1974, the real year,
or the time that god made the first
pterodactyls fly. Junk City is so big
it could cover the living room rug.
Buildings made out of tin foil
catch on fire.

In one dream the first president's name was Junk Washington
and he put out the fire from the other dream,
It was like that. I got older,
and Greg got older,
making Junk City so big that we started building it
under the ocean like a tunnel
using all the ocean junk like tangled seaweed
and rotted shark's teeth, rusted jewels
from a pirate's treasure chest. We made castles
for eels and crowns for mermaids
out of junk rubies and junk diamonds.
It was so good that I tried so hard
not to wake up, so hard did I hold my breath
that the tunnel gave way and water rushed in
so hot I didn't know whether it was cold or not.
But last night was different. I usually like to dream
my dreams awake to make them come true. It's like thinking
about Junk City so long you could move inside it,
and no one will ever call you back home again
and no one can make you leave it.

TOUGH LOVE

Management without waste
those early years of spotless marriage
when everything balanced
momentarily, bottled milk, muffins,
coffee on a checkered tablecloth
red & white & red
& white, everything a perfect symmetry,
I think of you watching me
through the kitchen hallway
through all the notions
of finding happiness
in early May, Arizona,
spring on Tennyson Street
when all that mattered
was how to save anything
in small amounts,
love or sex or jealousy.
Curiosity was enough,
like children playing
we meant for it to be fun—
the house as rudimentary
as a child's drawing of a house,
squares & windows & chimney
and the bright continuous yellow sun
that burned for days & days
until every desire was exhausted
and we lay asleep on the mattressed floor,
1972, listening to Dylan's love songs
over a game of chess and patchouli incense,
Honey, Darling, Sweetheart,
If we could have been as small as the waterspider

we could have walked on water too.
When the child was first born
he lay effortlessly on my flaccid belly
a matter of bulk and the branching of love,
tough love, against the seasons
against the weathering of marriage
at ordinary speed. Maybe it was something else
we were after with each exotic new act,
each meal of Bourgoignonne,
Ratatouille, all the purposeful waste
& crossed messages, words
which leave in their wake
only a conspiracy of silence
though, even now, there are nights wasted
with the radio on, staring
at the ceiling, not knowing
where I am or when. Only that it is autumn
and I am writing this down
from a place that is far away—
further than we imagined.

ONCE

I suffered a perfect departure
from a lover in winter.
We drove for hours into the frozen night
till daylight. There was nothing
more to say,
though we both realized the necessity
of that progression
through darkness into morning.
Since then, I've left many letters
unopened, forgiven some,
and written countless others
about infidelity in austere landscapes.
Goodbye to old confidences,
those imagined and real, both the same.
I was beginning to believe in them
and myself a lost child gladdened
by the name of any known street.
If daily life is the distance
between desire and arrival,
these words must be telegrams,
I was beginning to believe in them
and myself tumbling on endlessly
drumming up bad weather.

TALK

If it's requited, it's not
love, she says. My friend
is pushing forty
and has traded in the ornaments
of youth for flat statement.
Even the atmosphere
in her talcum-pink apartment
testifies to this: We waste the years
no matter what we waste them on,
and she has pictures
enough in her head
and records to conjure up the face
of any true fool she's
fallen for. There are few
certitudes for sure,
she knows; all the rest is luck.
But she is smart,
my friend is.
All the messages magneted
to the refrigerator promise
tomorrow she will give up
this & that, put on her best
late sixties off-the-shoulder dress,
then walk down to the club
like some voodoo Cinderella
looking for a quick game
of liars dice and a face
specific as any
she remembers.
It's a creed: To fall
is all there is,

to fall is everything
and then remember.

COUNTING ON ONE HAND

*It's because they are in love
that everything is about to go wrong.*
—Jean-Luc Godard

All my friends are having troubles
with their lovers. It's not
only a problem of men
and women married for years against
unlimited possibilities of desire.

            Between here & there
in barlight anything is cinematic.
He walks toward her in slow motion
and what is said or not
is something to think about
on those other nights
when there's no firewood or leftover
French Cuisine or anything
not domestic like sex or groceries.

            Tonight in a single bed
I count all the men I've ever loved
on one hand, the other is reserved for myself,
I test each bitten fingernail—
test it for flexibility, for strength. The phone rings;

my friends are having troubles with their lovers.
It's what we share and can't talk away
because defeat and sex should be kept
secret as the names of boys we had superimposed
over our own in school lined notebooks,

[12]

blurred to abstraction, or like the words
of love letters we memorized
only to forget what they meant:
warmth & resignation, sex & groceries.

          The combinations
stagger, a thousand ragged edges coming home
from the latest French film
where each lover believed himself
misunderstood as their hands disengaged
under the neon sign of the Porte d'Auteuil
and they parted in the still shot
of separate moonlight.

If all my friends are victims
and me, what about that other one
who turns his head of cold light,
his heels clicking away
into a choreography
of well timed maneuvers. You know,
the one we always talk about.

IS IT YOU

This miserable weather
just keeps repeating itself
in this city, in this rented room
where sometimes the phone rings
once then stops. Is it you?
If you were here
we could make it all public,
walk out to the Embarcadero
conjuring fiery death
at the arcade's Deathtrap.
Your shoes black and slick
as a policeman's, confident
you haven't had a drink
in months. And still
it means the world to me
when you write there are
places you long to return to, patterns
on pillowcases you remember
as specifically as the last time
we lifted our heads from them.

Even now, the one photo
I keep of you scans me
everywhere, grinning
like a hologram.
Or maybe this is only
an illusion of shelter—
to lie here naked
while between us
there is space enough
for entire zones of bereavement.

I am here. And is that you
sitting pretty
with your swiss army knife
tucked into your pocket
and your detective's hat
and your hoodlum's jacket
singing: *Throw me into the city*
naked and watch me fly.
The kind of hero
who drowns but never dies.

Who drowns
through the repertoire
of the city's cold trance
into a fanfare
of flourescent lights
and photo booths;
flimsy as the music
that says something plain
and stupid we never imagined
we could believe in
but sat hypnotized
in the late light
of last summer, listening
to ourselves think
like a radio
caught between two stations
dumb and tuneless
humming along with this romance
for what we can't have
and don't want
and want—all those threatening
and sweet things that get us through
the one and only final nights.

SIGNIFICANT OTHERS

At The Rite Spot, a corner bar
between Folsum and 17th, I'm caught
again half drunk in mid-
sentence between Tuesday
and the story of his life
these days, this oriental stranger
who shines paper
or something for a living.
Snakeskin shirt and eyes,
ruby studded lapel, he's jazzed
on something not for sale,
something I get if
I go with him
and slow dance to the rusted music
on the jukebox, if I
answer his senseless come-ons
about love. Who knows.
Maybe I dress like I should
go with strangers up and down
the lumpy spine
of the city
praying to the marquee
of light at The Roxy
where they're featuring
Marilyn Monroe in her last year
bolt-upright with fright
and sleeplessness,
plump and almost ripe.
The drunker he gets
the more he babbles
about Japan

where the symbol for suicide
is the cherry blossom:
Live briefly but gloriously.
Who has time
for early warnings
for the fur and diamond aura
of movie stars, for the traffic
and receipts. She died by accident.
Love, isn't there another
subject? Another place
to go without sleep?
Come morning, he'll guide
my American heart and portable shoulders
and walk me down
to the vacant Pacific
where ocean liners
are getting ready
to disembark. This side,
the highway is stalled
in its recent memory
of evenings when things run out:
the heart fails, sleep seizes
the wheel, the disappointed
lovers and insomniacs. Saturated,
he rubs his belly
like a stupid Buddha, fluffs out
his lap and calls me over. It's obvious,
he doesn't have to ask, he
knows my type.

BECAUSE ALL BOUNDARIES ARE
SUBJECT TO SLOW CHANGE

The boatless, bankless horizon
before us is open without us.

With the smallest housefly
returning to circle our heads

scrubbing its iridescent eyes
the "near future" hovers

as we lie content, side by side,
in the single bed

where I've begun to sleep alone.
To admit it is anything more would imply

other separations: chin, shoulder,
my index finger grazing the surface of your thigh

till you know I'm ready again
and we wade in slowly

like swimmers in the dark
depending on moonlight

or anything that distinguishes
shoreline from water.

WHAT I CAN'T SAY

All evening we've been walking, talking about Hemingway:
how a man could sit for hours in a darkened cafe
with a glass of brandy and somehow
believe he is still alive,
his face scarred by the shadows of leaves
a tree made against an electric light.

Your mother did not mean for you to come home
in the middle of the morning,
drapes still drawn, her in her nightgown
as if she were still sleeping, her fingernails
and round mouth painted perfectly.
Because you were a child you lay beside her.

Now you rest against someone's stone fence
and between us is your sadness
I have studied with a lover's scrutiny,
though we're not lovers
under this half-moonless summer's sky.

Because you were a child, you say
you have never visited your mother's grave
and imagine it an emptiness in the earth
where forever the dead are like water
seeking their own level.

I am almost her age then:
I want to say that courage is only
the putting aside of imagination.

It's not exactly like falling in love
again with a boy of eighteen
to almost believe I can tell him everything
because the darkness makes us equal
and there's something sexual about protection.

TO MICHAEL BACK IN PRISON

On second thought, one year might be time
enough to make you want to go back—
back home, Michael, not that rented room
you took me to eager and shy and
swearing I was your first woman
in six years, as if I would disbelieve you,
interrogate you as you held me down naked
against the naked mattress and had me confess
you hadn't forgotten anything.
Again and again, my favorite fantasy
of deprivation come true
in which I am the abundance,
the shot of heroin back into your vein.
Michael, you were so naked
I had to give you everything:
the pots and plants, the pillow, the hammer and the iron,
the whole neon hallucination of the city night
planet of barlights and convenience stores,
electronic bank tellers. *We're living in the future,*
you said. The promise and the wings.
The stone conciliation with this world
which cannot guarantee to keep you clean
or free from pain or the desire
to leave it again.
I think we spent three days in that room
with one of everything; the blue washcloth
that cleaned our genitals and faces,
dried the pot we used to cook the eggs
until we were both prisoners of this spare economy
and grace, masochists or saints.
If I could hold you now, I'd say I'm sorry

I didn't love either of us
enough to stop the predictable fear
we will re-enter our lives the only way
we ever have, by flight and resignation,
and we have. You're back home in prison tonight,
while I trace the perimeter of these rooms
and rest awhile on that pillow
that leaks feathers with small flights
of information, dream omens
to predict the pure white sleep
of heroin, fine yeast of sex.
I wash the dishes; I put on your torn jeans
and roll up the cuffs, put my hands in your pockets
and hold myself.

I CONFESS

Because fantasy has no gravity
and old boyfriends are like a row
of motels without marriage,
I sit in my living room of stale perfume,
late movies for a background,
fondling the biography of a 40's actor
gone wrong. Now dead,
his life a public property,
they can say what they want,
the way you do about old boyfriends,
the one who looked so much like Montgomery Clift
people stopped him at luncheonettes:
"Don't I know you from some war?"
And he made me feel as glamorous
as Elizabeth Taylor, a debutante
when so obviously I wasn't,
and our own famous story, obviously
nothing more than a grade-B fantasy
run to death. And then
there was *The Convict I Loved;*
of all my old boyfriends for only one
or two would I lay myself down in the gutter,
could I imagine confessing anything—
and then emerging like the convict
on the front page who admitted
hating himself every minute of his life,
and the Judge who pronounced
"But everyone's terrific at hindsight."
And he was right: who's to say who's wrong
or who'll have the last word?
Who's to say if we'll be remembered, like Monty,

for being a lousy lover or having bad credit?
Or would we, maybe, be spared
to float down pleasure river forever,
meeting old boyfriends unexpectedly
in the emergency room of dreams?
Who's to say what's to become of the past—
those perfectly edited stories,
all those histories of false confessions. . . .
I'd rather watch it on the movies,
sitting faithfully on my mauve sofa
like some Hollywood guru of self-denial,
of glamour & passion gone wrong, or just gone.

FOR MY THERAPIST

On the subject of my pain.
First of all it is not an object. I put my finger
on the center of an imaginary lightly dotted square
like a road map's D-5, parallel to my hip bones.
It doesn't smell like anything except maybe a place
where a rainstorm has evaporated on black asphalt.
My son's been there, but he was too small
to remember. We used to share the same symbols
for mountain peaks and time zones. He was smaller
                    than a green fist
of space set aside for a park. We were healthier together.

Once I had a lover who said he could feel it like a spider.
His mother was a suicide so I believed him.
A one-car, high-speed, late-night accident. I held my breath
while coming. I didn't want him to know too much
about me, to peel back the fabric of skin & lace & web.
To know the exact spot.

I know you think I'm not being specific enough when addressing
the subject of my pain. That I'm not saying Dear Pain:
you are useful in my love.

I've done the other exercise for pain
five times today and it still comes out the same.
The right hand holds
all the good memories,
all the ex-pretty, the ex-years,
the mock-empty christmas gifts
department stores showcase in their windows.
The left hand rattles

the dulled silver of the train;
the noise the pain makes
as it grinds over the track
can lull a race track loser to sleep
with only train fare home.

I swear, for a small amount
of morphine, for the liquor-slicked throat of anyone,
for the flesh and the light, I'd retreat into the tunnel.
The pain which is dedicated to me would perfectly fold
into itself, and we would both sleep side by side
like indifferent parallel necessary mates
navigating our way across the country.

Two

A Life of Lives

THE COAT

The first time I noticed the blue
on the white snow was the day
my mother found a twenty dollar bill
on the way to the subway
and cautioned me to walk always
with my head to the ground
if I ever expected to find anything
in this world for free.
It was the first day my father wore
the enormous brown overcoat,
all he had left of his dead brother,
the coat I was afraid of
because I believed my father
walked everywhere like a ventriloquist
wisecracking to his fat unfunny brother
like they always had
on Sundays around the kitchen table
while my mother basted the chicken
or peeled the potatoes.
It was New Year's day, 1961,
the upside down year I turned over
& over again on the cover of Mad Magazine
while my father got drunk
on the subway and joked & cried
for his brother who he would
never see again, not for *Auld Lang Syne*,
not for all the coming emptiness
of 1961 which turns over & over
like my uncle's inscrutable riddle
about the weight of gold or feathers
that I had to answer

before he'd give me a silver dollar
or a chocolate kiss.
On the first day of 1961
my father cried on the subway
as my mother took the whole family
to see Natalie Wood & Warren Beatty
fall in love in a small town in Kansas
in a time my mother said she could remember,
the brief good years before the Depression.
She was my age then, thirteen.
On January 1, 1961, it was so cold
on the balcony of the Loews Valencia
my mother allowed my father
to give me a sip of the brown liquor
and then another & another
as Natalie Wood ran hysterical,
from a classroom, after losing her first love
and reading a passage
from Intimations of Immortality,
words about loss and strength
I memorized as the theatre went dark again
and we all rode home a little drunk
& silent in the artificial midnight
lighting of the IRT where I wrote my first poem
and my mother counted her change like feathers or gold
and my father fell asleep on her shoulder
snoring with his ghostly brown coat wrapped around them.

SOMETHING IN PUBLIC

I never met the man
who carved and painted
twin wolverines
floating on a sky blue wall
over my parents' bed.
Father explains,
to be crazy, really crazy,
you do something in public,
and someone notices, takes you away.
Privately, at the Poughkeepsie Hospital
for the Insane my uncle paints
war horses with open nostrils
and bloody eyes. All he has left,
remembrance and pain,
he divides into his separate selves
like neighbors who
having argued years before
never violate their silent
agreement not to give in.
To forgive but not forget is hell,
he says, and my father agrees
to forget would be much better
than this silent frenzy
of chiseled wood—all detail.
And now he can remember
only the details:
Forty years ago his large mother
crushed her breasts as she leaned
from her second story landing
to watch her grown son
stone the windows of Delancey Street

till the sirens came
and the wolves wandered
confused in broad daylight.

THE ELECTRIC CHAIR

It was known as the Dance Hall by some who witnessed the executions. The straining of the body against the straps holding a man through the electric current gave a ghastly simulation of life.
PLAQUE ON FIRST ELECTRIC CHAIR

That morning the laundry
had been sprawled
over the floor.
I heard a car screech
outside, sounding like my mother
crying I should leave
for school or go away.
My father with his fist
on the table;
the green bottle
on the table.

Death was instantaneous.
Remembering this, once
I walked through a trailer,
a child among two rows
of school children
wearing a yellow and pink carnation
made from tissue paper.
Helpless as my imagining

of burnt flesh, I learned
one man's request
for a white shirt
and tie so he could "die stately,"
and in my imagining
willful, papery,
sacramental.

There was an exhibition
of punishment:
the great wooden chair
with pinioning straps,
and a wax man
with a mustache
and clear blue eyes
alive enough to make
a child step back.
Someone explained
how the executioner
fits one white disc
to the calf of the leg
another to the crown
of the head.
Someone flicks a switch.

There was a particular sadness
in the child's invention
I could will myself
never to be surprised
or sorry or dead,
rather it was a promise
to remain always serious and good.
What I traced in my looseleaf,
was the stiff claw of a blackbird,
a stone skipping like a rabbit
escaping on the surface.

Above, other figures
and something white
disappearing behind white hills.

For fear of it, or
for love and punishment
I wanted finally to sit
on the oaken chair,
for exhaustion and danger,
the message of reprieve
from the parents
arriving just in time,
but my ghost, already separate,
masquerading above me
in spiteful victory
and judgment for us all.

But I was seven or eight,
and still afraid
of killing someone
and that strange
consentless dance
that follows.
That night I saw
my mother
lying on the couch,
her sleeve torn
to the elbow,
telling me to go back
to bed or look away.
The draperies flourished
their patterned grotesquery
inviting me to their corner.
Go stand in the corner.
I switched on the light
my father's green face

melted to the table,
then I switched on the light.

TOKEN

My mother keeps an artificial wallet
in her pocketbook to fool the hoodlums of the city.
Thick with newspaper torn into money,
it is the wallet not chained
to the inner security zipper.
FUCK YOU it says on the transparent plastic folder
for credit cards and photos of loved ones.
FUCK YOU on the window for identification.
In case of emergency, she carries it everywhere
invisibly as the belief in god
or knowledge of karate. Any god can tell you this,
she knows, that everything she's ever saved
is just so much dinero in the sky,
small change to the sun.
But to ride the subways in the heavy metallic hour
before the rush, as the train burrows
from one man-made darkness into another,
between flourescent stations
yellowed to the color of the moon—
everyone needs something besides
themselves to conceal for ransom.

THE SURFACE OF THE HEART

Her mother named her Hilda and Hinde
and later forgot which one she chose. But she
had no feeling for anything,
chest burning, hands frozen to the pillow,
and it was no dream that morning she woke up
in the diphtheria dark mentholated room
where her father spoke to the leeches
like pets while her brothers
died choking beside her—
what would happen to *her,* in a few days,
forever, she heard her father say in the way
that meant *surprise.* Years ago, *everything happened.*
Now it doesn't matter, she says,
grateful for nothing unexpected in this year.
If the heart had its sensitive surface exposed—
I think about my mother near her 60th year—
it would be a beautiful error,
and dangerous. My mother keeps her silence.
And like the African tribe that kept
no record of its births, its deaths,
she doesn't care to know how old she is.

THIRTY-FIVE

My parents comfortably retired
in Miami, the afterlife
for Jews who believe
in no afterlife.
My son, the blond whiz
of abstract third grade math.
Chicken gizzards on the counter
longing to become
the soup. Fingers & toes &
fingers, room for improvement
& wings. Plus some added to others. 35
is the first age I remember my mother at.
Her shoulders thick as potatoes
boiling over plaid shoulderless
dresses in summer, hoarding in her bosom
the recipe for middle age which begins:
There are no early warnings and ends
*Nothing above eye level is worth
your concern* . . . but, oh, to be
the child spinning round and round
in the city park until trees become
pigeons become messages saying *Welcome
Back*. Proof that everything
is either real or not. But if 35
to 35 my mother and I sat spliced
together on the same park bench
watching our children at play,
she might imagine me as someone
random, going and coming
gazing above the level of trees,
while my son counts jet sparrows

horizon to horizon—counts the splinters
in broken walking sticks. *Numbers For Sale*
he'll yell, *Cheap!*

        This American language, she'll think,
then call me over, and we would almost recognize
ourselves as instant versions
of each other. She'd signal, I'd wink
or maybe spin the chicken back
until everything added up to egg,
to 35, a number in the middle
of the universe of centrifical force,
an early warning that half
of everything is either real
or not, the rest the vapor
that boils away, twice removed
from your childhood broth.

WALKING WITH MY SON

Bending to the ground
he recognizes the way
the earth forms crevices
of meaning, calligraphy
from which lines
of ants emerge, parading.
Then what to make
of the cardinal's wing,
fanned and still
in the new grass, and is it
true that what we eat
lives inside us,
somehow whole—
as I was aware,
not by its sound,
but by the thinking:
the creek's turning
in the bushes nearby—
those things we know
by imagination,
to illustrate the unexplained.
Later, walking back
beneath the cool
north light, Bodi
crushes ants, makes
up stories we take home:
the trees' breath
in his hair, the wing
red in his pocket.

SUGAR

He was three years old
and growing smaller.
Seven hours in a coma
while the nurses probed
his tense, white skin,
till the silvery life
of electrolytes and insulin
kicked in.
                    He'll make it.
I asked for a Valium
and stepped outside
where the question moon
suggested vertigo
beyond blood numbers,
digital, a wind
beyond those cubicles
of artificial light.
Diabetes Mellitus.
We'll make it.
Breathe it in,
the doctor said without apology,
put it in your lungs.

                    We moved
around some, got adjusted.
Fragrant autumn nights
he leaves the back door open.
He says he likes
the way it looks
to let the outside in,
to see nothing but

the glow-in-the-dark
astronaut poster
and the luminous earth
from where he falls
gracefully through space.
Isn't it beautiful, he says,
to be *almost* blind.
And he's fine now,
I can say it; even when
I touch his eleven year old
needle-toughened skin,
I only feel my *own*
fear.
                    It's me
who's growing smaller,
wondering how he sees
me by day
as he drifts slowly
down the hill alone
on his way to school,
waving to me
as though my face
were the earth,
and he the luminous astronaut
floating beyond
the gravity of home.

NO

As I walk back from the yard sale,
a five dollar human skull in newspaper
inside my shopping bag,
I'm following this man
who struts angrily in front of me
with a warped bicycle tire
clutched like a twisted universe
beneath a tanned and oiled bicep;
it is almost autumn
as he parts the traffic
with his body, kicks his dog,
smartasses his lingerie-ad girlfriend,
parades his private symptoms
down public streets
like a slow walking ambulance,
maybe remembering, as I do,
the moon of last night
dissolving in the sky
like a bitter aspirin and all
the visible stars and galaxies
just a junkyard of bones,
just another reason to light a cigarette,
to say No and Why Not—Why not
with our five dollar skulls,
our superfluous souls,
and heaven, at best,
only a milky blue illusion
anesthetized by sky.

OCTOBER

They are all beautiful
pearls, even the homely ones,
walking to the schoolyard
at the beginning of their day,
sleepy or confused, as though
all promise of the future lay
obligated in their bodies.

Their fears, their laughter
all invite as pretext
that dark monarchy which
labors: the cloud
within the pearl, the loss,
the emptied street, almost
illusory by now. And then

the surface: as before sunrise,
the great sky with its
aspect of twilight.

WALKING OUT INTO A STORM

Into an emergency which is everywhere
safe and impersonal,

past the woman whose baby
was due last Thursday

who watches us through her picture window
still heavy bellied in her blue tunic

and the elderly couple
home from the clinic

their windows already darkened to the color
of the sky. I wish I knew the names

of everything in danger,
like those moist skinned amphibians,

salamanders, who always emerged
magically after a summer's storm.

My brother and I collected them
and let them live awhile in shoeboxes

with jar lids full of water and wilted lettuce;
each time one died it was a sacrifice we promised

not to make again. It was said
that they lived in fire,

as here in the desert in the summer
the dry culverts ready themselves

for the water's weight. I felt
the abundance of this once when

I went out to make love
in the enclosure of a desert downpour.

It was something to praise. Simply,
like a good cry after a birth

or a broken heart, or a cup of water,
cold, at the end of summer.

WEEKDAY MATINEES

I

By twilight every ghost lover combines
to make up this view outside my window,
this San Francisco fog:
condensed atmosphere mangled by telephone wires
and low flying jets. Every outline blended
in quicksilver dusk, smoothed by shadow
while the droplet features of old lovers
run languidly down the glass.
                    They could be
the watery eyes of Christ that once followed me
through a stranger's room, a man I'd just met
and made love to in a canopied bed of white lace.
The face of Christ plastered everywhere,
delicately framed on the dresser,
painted in dayglow on the walls. Afterwards,
he lit a candle until everything disappeared
into the flickering images you barely see passing by
a drive-in movie on a moonlit highway . . .
And still I can't remember his face
as I dressed and left
to catch the downtown weekday matinee.

II

People are talking to the movie
in this theatre of skipped seats,
the stained velvet upholstery,
where 75¢ gets you two features
and a luminous darkness.
Goddam Bitch babbles the fat man

from a back row to the alcoholic floozabel
on the screen. He'll never let any woman
treat him like that. Someone else mumbles
about Jesus: *Jesus Christ* in a voice rusted
and distant as the barely audible soundtrack—

                Fat City: about a failed boxer
a man who attached himself,
too late, to the wrong future.
It's also about the urban poor.
The floor creaks when the fat man
gets up to buy more popcorn. The floozy
packs her black boyfriend's clothes
in the liquor store carton because
he's back in prison now and she's not eating anymore
just drinking Thunderbird. When she tries
to get out of bed, she keeps falling back.
Nobody moves. Nobody laughs at the funny parts.

III

It gets easier.

In my bed, by myself, I love
the neighbor's clarinet practice
from the next apartment, the same woman
who by daylight stops me on the street,
shows me her photographs, those vague
double exposed postures of her mother
rising three times from her dying body
or Saint Peter blowing a golden horn.
She has even photographed Satan
who she says picks after her from the radio
and t.v., who, she says, most people
can believe in without ever having
seen him, a maze of faces and blue light,

in the photograph she keeps tucked
in her pocketbook that also resembles
this city at night as it loses itself
in a featherbed romance of fog
where men and women and invisible passages
weave their light together with the fading light
and without asking we close our blinds against one another
until everything disappears, and we sleep.

EAGLE 21

The dwellings of Southern Texas
shimmy by me: The hand lettered facade
of Sammy's Country Store & Art Gallery,
laundry waving like flags
of surrender from all those
whose houses face the tracks
that line America: a world
of lost dogs, graveyards,
and abandoned cars
where skinny grazing horses
repeat themselves
like the Hank Williams' refrain
we sang along to last night
when the generators died
between Texarcana,
Texas and Texarcana, Arkansas.
Floating on anonymous,
rusted ribs, it was easy
to sing of loneliness,
to start from anywhere
and introduce ourselves:
Diesel Driver, Crime Reporter,
and three-year-old Benjamin
who swore he saw a ghost
when the lights went out
and a milk-white nightgown
walked by in the moonlight.
"I want to go home," he cried.
Not me, just beginning to belong—
recognizing the strangeness
of every stranger's face as my own,

a face in a window,
one of those I used to wave to
when a train orbiting
seemed nothing less than a miracle—
that dimly lit planet
with its glassed-in aliens.
Better to be one of those who move,
while still, turning pages
in the complimentary magazine
whose back cover features
a soaring silver eagle advertising,
NOT EVERYONE WAS MEANT TO FLY.
And I agree with everyone
sitting by me: All those
adlibbing lyrics
to a couple of untuned guitars,
something about vacancy
& horses—an emergency
plausible enough
to pull out the lever
from the windows
& watch the ghosts
of morning
tumble back in.

A LIFE OF LIVES

It was an ordinary
late afternoon outing:
February, San Francisco
when fog locks the passersby
in sleep-walking tempo;
where, from Safeway's parking lot,
endangered gypsy children
were selling bags
of garlic, icons
from another world, & young
Hispanic men lined up great
works of art on velvet.

From a small dirt island—
a concrete bench, a tree—
a man rose up; his face & body
effaced by a gray film of earth.
Merging into traffic,
he reminded me
of a Russian artist's
Anti-Christ, a gaunt
& joyless man beyond
a warm place for the night,
another drink, or a fix
of anything to set
the world all right.

And that was it.
I got my groceries, I paid,
I trudged downhill to my apartment
that overlooks the freeway,

the bay windows'
mirrors reflecting
how boneless inside
everything is:
The city's concrete boulevards
& troubled roads, and in the casual
spectacle of winter clad people,
a life of lives, wafting
bravely down the streets
where character is no more
than visible fate,
a face in the crowd
erasing himself,
forgiving me as I look.

The National Poetry Series 1986

Junk City

Barbara Anderson
Selected by Robert Pinsky/Persea Books

Cardinals in the Ice Age

John Engels
Selected by Philip Levine/Graywolf Press

Little Star

Mark Halliday
Selected by Heather McHugh/William Morrow & Co.

Cities in Motion

Sylvia Moss
Selected by Derek Walcott/University of Illinois Press

Red Roads

Charlie Smith
Selected by Stanley Kunitz/E.P. Dutton

The National Poetry Series was established in 1978 to publish five collections of poetry annually through five participating publishers. The manuscripts are selected by five poets of national reputation. Publication is funded by James A. Michener, Edward J. Piszek, The Copernicas Society of America, The National Endowment for the Arts, The Friends of the National Poetry Series, and the five publishers—E.P. Dutton, Graywolf Press, William Morrow & Co., Persea Books, and The University of Illinois Press.